THE PROM DRESS ROOM

Sandy Hazlett

ANAMCARA PRESS

ANAMCARA PRESS
P.O. Box 442072
Lawrence, KS 66044
www.anamcara-press.com

Copyright © Sandy Hazlett, 2015
Illustrations by Sandy Hazlett

The Prom Dress Room was previously published
in the Coal City Review, Issue 36, 2015
Brian Daldorph, editor.

ISBN: 978-1-941237-05-2

All rights reserved.
No part of this publication may be reproduced, stored in a retrieval system,
or transmitted in any form or by any mechanical recording or otherwise,
without prior written permission of the copyright owner.

Printed in the United States of America

*Profits from the sale of the Prom Dress Room go to
the Social Service League of Lawrence, Kansas*

Contents

Foreword

The Story Behind *The Prom Dress Room*

3D Red

Crystal Leaf

Diamond Straps

Homemade Sparkling Peach

Blue Velvet Saks

Disco Ariadne

Blush

Orchidaceae

Solitaire

Footnotes

FOREWORD

Sandy Hazlett's *The Prom Dress Room* is a collection of stories about women coming of age while navigating cultural, family and community dangers and daring possibilities. In telling the tales of dresses and their owners, Hazlett speaks to the many ways in which young women can be silenced or even have their greatest passions erased as well as the small but holy moments of redemption that ripple out across wounded lives. From one who says, "I became the fallen diamond strap"" to another who tells us, "We get by with a moderately hemmed life," Hazlett sings the pulse of finding, losing and reclaiming identity and even grace. The poems are sublime, fierce, musical, and daring, and the whimsical drawings convey hope and fear in their many guises. This is a superb collection of poems, stories and images that illuminates real lives in and well beyond prom dresses.

~Caryn Mirriam-Goldberg, 2009-13 Kansas Poet Laureate

THE STORY BEHIND *THE PROM DRESS ROOM*

In Lawrence, Kansas, there is a unique thrift shop called The Social Service League, which sells clothing, books, and household items and serves as a dynamic community hub. Upstairs, in its old stone building, the League has a room full of donated formal dresses which are given to young women to wear to their prom.

One winter I volunteered to clean and organize the dresses. As I sorted through their colorful variety, they began to tell their stories: Who wore this dress? What was her life like? Who would she become? Each week I took one dress home, made my amateur ink drawing, colored it in with fat pencils, and wrote the story of the dress and the young woman who wore it to prom. The result is this collection of nine illustrations and poems, *The Prom Dress Room*.

SDH
Lawrence, Kansas
May 2015

3D Red

I am venous, anoxic,
iridescent blue/red running under skin.
Deep in shadow and shimmer,
I skim the Andes at sunset,
the rib of a fallen prey.

I am flamenco sumac, autumn viburnum,
shifting fault lines in the earth's core,
glint of sun off a Maori's oar,
red velvet cake under crystal dome,
a perfect glass of port.

Along my back runs an undulant sash,
quiver slant tied to the center fold,
a yawl's rudder trail. Cilia, flagella,
evolution of an armored tail,
princess and dragon rustling as one
down the hewn stone stair.

I am Maillol's Méditerranée,
thick molded thighs,
midnight hair waving on white skin,
mottled as the dress.
We are cut from the same bolt.

I hiss at my mother and baffle my father.
I will study erythrocytes under glass,
perfect dissections, pinned veins on wax.
I will go to medical school, become a surgeon,
master the boney hardness of life.

I marry three men, two Harrys and a Martin.
I leave each one.
My two girls grow to despise me.
I was not made for this man's world.

I set my glare for the one who could be my match.
There are no mirrors here, no stone
but you can almost hear
the hiss of snakes upon my brow.

Prom Dress Room
3D Red

Crystal Leaf

I hold the center close to my body,
skin soft and thin blurs the edge of cloth,
yellow like tallow, all potential flame.
I am surrounded by crystal leaves,
a Norwegian wood in early winter,
floating over secret folds,
a hint of falling,
falling green leaves.

My dancing ivory ground is the full moon
when no one is watching,
milkweed seed, soft snow.
Hush, hush, the sound of my skirt
against bare legs,
above lightly treading toes.

I am the oldest. I have a younger brother and two younger sisters.
My mother is bruised and quiet. She drinks sherry most days,
sleeps on the sofa or in her room with the door closed.
I have my own room. I am not allowed to lock my door.
My father is big and bristly. At night he comes to me,
pushes against me, covers my mouth,
insists in whiskery whispers, "this is our special secret."
Crying stays inside me, close to me,
slippery like tallow, wet and warm,
wrapped in rage until released to run over the forest floor.
I have not spoken to them in years.
I often wonder about my sisters.

I am a teacher of children in the first grade.
I hold them close, show them how to be safe,
how to see beauty if you know where to look,
how to shimmer without anyone
saying no, saying stop, saying don't.
I never marry.
I live alone.
I live for my first grade children,
for their shine.

The Prom Dress Room
Crystal Leaf

Prom Dress Room
Diamond straps

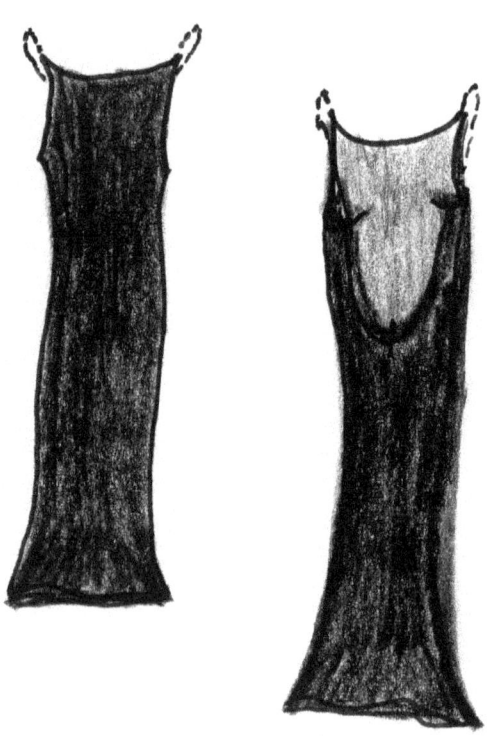

Diamond Straps

I mimic Madame X, sleek black with diamond studded straps.

I model the memory of the outrageous slip, off the shoulder,
the shock of it, Sargent's shame.

I wear my diamonds as they were repainted,
high and wide as my dreams.

I step elegantly into the future,
simple, stately, all line, no commotion,
poise, whispers, silence.

I hide in blackness turned in, no outward ceremony.
It is a matter of state. I will make my mark upon the world.

I give my valedictory address
overcome with the subtle hint that this,
this now, is the best it would ever be.

Within the year I drop out of college,
sit for days on the sofa,
solemn and suicidal.
There is no recovery. I am sent away.

I survive, barely, with the mark of mental illness,
a bit of hope, some surrender, more bitterness.
It never does get any better than that.

I become the fallen diamond strap.

Homemade
sparkling
Peach

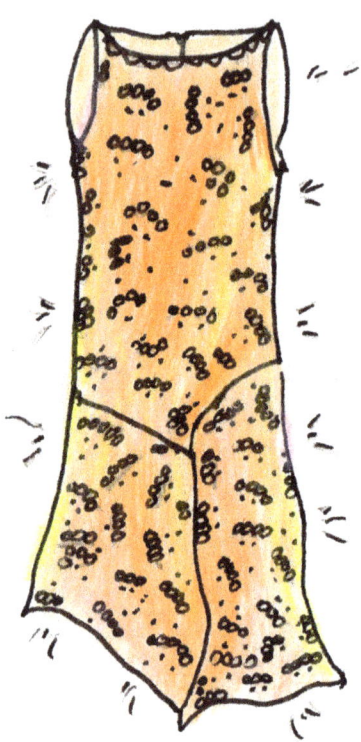

Homemade Sparkling Peach

I have gone gaudy at Hobby Lobby.
I have something to prove
and I mean to show them.
All sanguine and sequins,
I rush against running out,
running out of money, running out of time.
I hear my mother's fears.
How much can I spend and still look ravishing,
(because I will look ravishing)
in my dress for the prom?
I am self made and secure,
a 4H trained seamstress to boot.
I go for the vocal bolt,
fabric that confesses, calls,
and happens to be on sale.
A copy of a pattern
to tweak to my size, trim an edge,
I am on it.
My name is Sparkle, I go for the gold
bric-a-brac around my neck.
I keep myself above it, make it short, lots of leg.
I walk into a room like the sunrise.
I will become an entrepreneur,
import fabric and handcrafts from the Silk Road.
I marry a Presbyterian minister. I know it seems odd
but he indulges me.
We get by with a moderately hemmed life.
I make our lives into the future.
For my daughter, I sew her dress for the prom.

Blue Velvet
Saks

Blue Velvet Saks

I am the rich girl, deep in blue velvet Saks and satin,
the Mediterranean's evening sea,
cobalt and lapis lazuli.
I am the silent sapphire of Crater Lake,
the edge of night on the tallgrass prairie.
I am the plume of the Aurora, the infinite cerulean sky.

Within the body of this blue,
I am more manly than you would know
by my graceful step.
I am Tarzan on the playground.
I man the oars and come to the rescue.

Into this depth of blue
I become homeless
to earth and sky.
I live fluid,
just above the meniscus,
just shy of surface tension.
I am both mast and siren.

Up before light, I swim. I swim miles every day,
away from gravity, levitation to the bones.
One, two, breathe. One, two, breathe.
My water waltz, my liquid meditation.

I will win a scholarship with my stroke.
I am Olympic material they say
but my times fall short.
It passes me by.
I arise ordinary, landed.
When my girls are six and nine,
I suffer an aneurysm and drown
while on vacation in Vancouver.

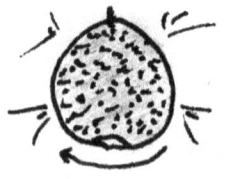

THE PROM DRESS Room
Disco Ariadne

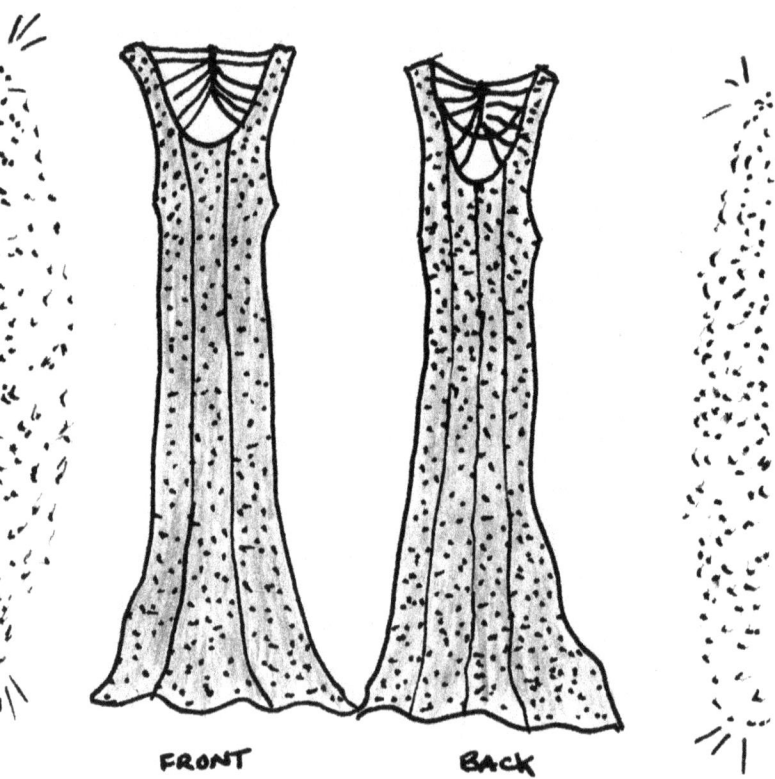

FRONT BACK

Disco Ariadne

I am glamorous,
revolving light,
reflecting outward,
along my sleek and slender form.
I carry silken thread
on the diamond studded
center of my back,
the thread that leads
out of the maze into the light.
I will save you from confusion,
from the darkness.
I celebrate my radiant participation
in the bacchanalian ball of the evening.
Before I step into the next world
of my adulthood let me shine now
so I may remember.

I will go to college. I will study astrophysics,
the web of the glittering universe.
I will meet a man who is an oceanographer.
We will marry and move to Woods Hole.

I shift my interest to the sea, to our coral reefs,
and I dive into the bioluminescent night.
One by one I watch them bleach and die,
mourn their extinguished light.
I can't save them
though they are made
from the same light as I.

Blush

I was the girlie girl,
bubble gum in silver foil,
My Little Pony,
Barbie doll,
pink haired troll.

My dress is heavy to wear.
Over a fine pink satin slip
lies its rosy sheath,
sewn with thousands of beads,
light-catching cylinders,
heavy enough to keep me grounded,
to keep me from leaping up,
leaping away.
The cowl draped down my back
becomes a pretty pack
when I finesse my leaving.

I will study painting.
I will make pastel swashes of dancers.
Over and over again I paint
ribbons and satin,
pointed toes,
the urgent power
of their delicate twirl.

I visit Degas at the Louvre,
the foot of Constantine in Rome,
Michelangelo's David.
I confess the most astonishing detail
of Annie Liebovitz in her studio
is the bare foot of Baryshnikov.

I have inherited the gene for Huntington's.
My life becomes heavy to wear.
I put my brushes down,
hold my older sister's hand,
and dance the rigid staccato of my limbs.

The Prom Dress Room
Blush

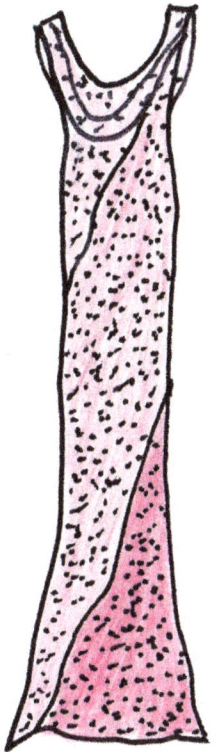
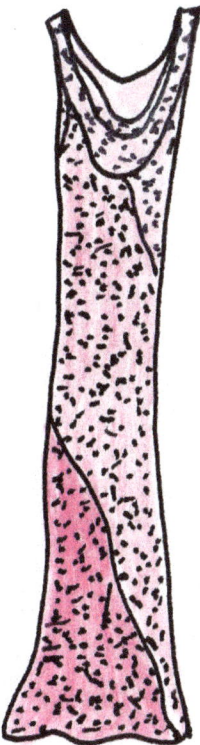

The Prom Dress Room
orchidaceae

Orchidaceae

This is not my testament.
I dropped the ball and sent out aerial roots
into the canopy of the Plant Queendom.
Perennial epiphyte, I am in the arms
of the mother, Pachamama.
Jaguar and puma pad below me
snarling upward their curl of sound.
I am blue green of the abundant river,
luminous, fecund, lethal.

This is my ovation.
On the shore of womanhood I search for our beginning,
when matriarchs joined hands in the circle of fathers,
when the blood that flowed from them,
the babies they bore,
the food they gathered and cooked at the fire,
their jungle of words that tied the band together,
all were lifted up in praise and placed in right communion.

I will scatter my studies between anthropology and ecology
until I hear the question, "should trees have standing?"
I will go to law school for environmental law.

I litigate for the world's women and children,
for the voiceless,
for the flora and fauna of the Amazonian Basin.
I screech and howl to protect the unprotected.
After all, it's a jungle out there.

The Prom Dress Worn
Solitaire

Solitaire

I am the winter prairie,
broom sedge, little bluestem,
coyote fur, a herding, lone, red heeler.
I am thin skinned, indecisive,
uncomfortable in crowds.
I melt into my dress.
I mimic flesh so I can blend in.
I keep it short so I can walk away.
Clubs, pearls, and lace at my waist,
two lines of thought, subtle decorum.
I am a pleated column.

I will go to nursing school,
join Doctors Without Borders,
travel to the Caucasus.
I will meet a handsome intern
who marries me when I become pregnant.
I raise his two sons. He never loves me.

We retire to Coral Gables, Florida.
The doctor dies peacefully in his reading chair.
I sneak cigarettes in the bathroom
and eat scrambled eggs with ketchup
because there is no one to tell me not to.
I have chronic catarrh and spit into the coconut tree.
In my pearl slippers on terra-cotta tile
I shuffle cards in a metal box
and play solitaire in the sunroom.

Footnotes

Many thanks to my readers and friends:
Caryn Mirriam-Goldberg, Elizabeth Schultz, Gary Lechliter, Brian Daldorph, Denise Low, Mary O'Connell, Ronda Miller, Nedra Rogers, Louise Smith, and Charlotte Pessoni.

Thanks also to Jean Ann Pike, former manager of the Social Service League, for all of her support, good humor, and the keys to the prom dress room.

To Jake Vail for his steadfast love and support.

"Blush" is dedicated to my dear friend, Gwen Wiens, and in memory of her sisters, Cindy Wiens and Jan Wiens.

"Blue Velvet Saks" is in memory of my grade school best friend, Debbie Williams.

www.ingramcontent.com/pod-product-compliance
Lightning Source LLC
Chambersburg PA
CBHW042000080526
44588CB00021B/2822